WHAT IT'S LIKE TO BE OLD

© Aladdin Books 1991

Design: Rob Hillier
Editors: Catherine Bradley, Jen Green
Picture research: Emma Krikler
Consultant: Angela Grunsell

The publishers would like to acknowledge that the photographs reproduced in this book have been posed by models or have been obtained from photographic agencies.

First published in the United States in 1992 by
Gloucester Press, 95 Madison Avenue, New York, NY 10016

Library of Congress Cataloging-in-Publication Data

Sanders, Pete.
     What it's like to be old / Peter Sanders.
          p.   cm. — (Let's talk about)
     Includes index.
     Summary: An introduction to what it's like to be old, physically and mentally, describing the joys and challenges of old age.
     ISBN 0-531-17372-0
     1. Aged—Juvenile literature. 2. Aging—Juvenile literature.
[1. Aged.   2. Old age.] I. Title.
HQ1061.S3115   1992
305.26—dc20   92-6683
                        CIP   AC

"LET'S TALK ABOUT"

WHAT IT'S LIKE TO BE OLD

PETE SANDERS

Gloucester Press

New York · London · Toronto · Sydney

"Why talk about what it's like to be old?"

Since opening this book and beginning to read it, you are slightly older than you were when you first picked it up. Throughout our lives, we change continually. You only have to think about how you looked five years ago to realize this.

There are now more elderly people in the world than ever. Most people in this country can expect to live out their old age. But being old is often not talked about, and is sometimes treated as a joke. Perhaps this is because it is thought of as the stage before death, and many people find this difficult to think about. Today old age may cover twenty or thirty years of our lives. This book will help you understand how enjoyable and challenging old age can be.

> We often imagine that elderly people cannot do lots of things. This need not be the case.

4

"What is old age?"

Old age means different things to different people. What seems old to you might appear young to one of your friends, to your teacher, or to a grandparent. You might try asking other people what they think of as old. Most people don't feel old just because they have lived for a certain number of years. Retirement from work is usually seen as the beginning of old age. In this country, the age of retirement is 60 or 65, but many people continue working for longer than that. In some countries people go on working long after their sixties. Their definition of old age may be very different from ours.

It is hard to believe, but if you are ten, you already look very old to someone much younger than yourself, like a baby brother or sister. To them everyone looks grown up.

7

"Why do some people live longer than others?"

Aging is part of the cycle of life, but nobody knows how long she or he will live. It seems that our bodies wear out at different rates. How we take care of ourselves can make a difference. Researchers have shown that the people who tend to live longer are those who are active, who exercise and eat healthily, and who can adapt to change.

In the last twenty years doctors have found out more about how to treat illnesses that people used to die of. Many people who live in Europe and the United States are likely to live into their seventies, or longer. This is not true for everyone in the world. There are many countries where medical help is not available, or is very expensive.

The habits you form now may affect your health and the quality of your life as you get older.

"What happens to us as we grow older?"

If you look at old photographs of members of your family, you can see how they have changed over the years. We will all look different by the time we reach old age. Some elderly people appear frightening to young children. Their bodies may have bent with age. If they have arthritis, the joints in their hands may be crooked. You know there is nothing to be frightened of. After all, wrinkles are just lines in the skin. As we grow old, our bodies change. Our muscles may become weaker, and our joints stiffen. Old people have to be careful when it is icy. If they fall, their bones may break more easily.

Old photographs can be interesting. As pictures of the same person at different stages in their life show, the way we look changes very much as we grow older.

Changes in the body are perfectly natural. But you can't always see what is happening. Some elderly people may not be able to smell or taste food as well as they could. This may mean that they are less interested in eating. Other elderly people may be hard of hearing. They may ask you to speak up or repeat what you have said. Some people have to do things more slowly than when they were younger. It is an easy mistake to think an older person can't do something, simply because he or she is taking a long time to do it. Sometimes older people's memories do not work very well. They may repeat themselves or interrupt you. They may no longer be used to conversation, especially if they live alone.

Though our bodies may change, our interests may not. Some older people find it difficult to be thought of as old. In our society we tend to expect old people to behave in a certain way. We often see elderly people as a group instead of as individuals. We presume they can't or shouldn't do certain things. This attitude is called ageism.

In some countries, elderly people are seen as being very special and wise, and are treated with respect. The gold tablets worn by these elders in Ghana, Africa, show their high status.

"Should older people be treated differently?"

Has anyone ever patted you on the head as though you were a five-year-old? If so, you might understand the frustration that elderly people feel when treated as though they are helpless or foolish. For instance, older people may need you to speak clearly if they are hard of hearing, but that doesn't mean they are stupid. Some elderly people are frail, and need special help and attention. But this is not the case with all elderly people. Often young people like to help older people. Sometimes this may mean that they rush in and do things for them, without checking whether help is needed. It may be that an old person needs no help at all to do many things.

Elderly people are often pleased when you have helped them. But just like you, there are times when they prefer to do things for themselves.

"How should I behave with older people?"

You already know something about ageism and how important it is to treat people as individuals. Most young people find it difficult to respect others simply because they have lived for a longer time. You may feel that some of the old people you know are very critical. They may not like your hairstyle, or the way you dress. They may say that you are noisy. They may seem very strict, and not allow you to do the things that other people let you do. They may also express racist or sexist views which they learned a long time ago, which you find difficult or boring to listen to.

If you get into conversation with an older person, you may find that you have many interests and happy memories in common. These pictures were taken eighty years apart.

It is important to remember how much society has changed over the last seventy years. Lots of the things that we take for granted now had not yet been invented. For instance, seventy years ago there were hardly any cars on the roads. There were no televisions, and few people had radios or telephones. Some elderly people find change difficult to accept. They may feel that things were better when they were young. Sometimes old people find today's attitudes strange, and today's manners casual or even rude.

It is important to try to understand how other people feel. You might try asking older people how they felt about the way they were expected to behave when they were your age. You may find they had some of the same feelings then that you have now. Young and old people often have a great deal to learn from each other. Ageism can create many kinds of problems. If we think of old people as merely old, we may well be missing out on the lifetime of skill and experience they have to offer.

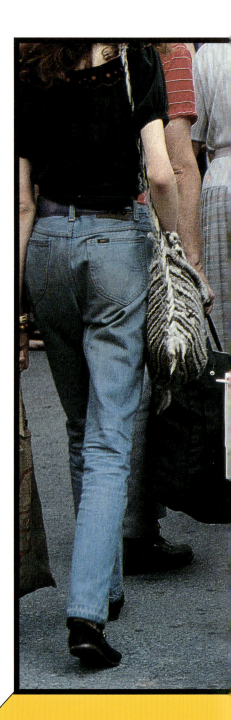

The lives of many elderly people are made much easier by new technology. But some may find modern electronic devices unfamiliar or even bewildering.

"What do people enjoy about being old?"

When people retire from work, they have more time in their lives to do other things. This can take some getting used to. Some couples find it odd to have so much time together, after a lifetime of being apart during the day.

Having the extra time means that most elderly people can choose how they spend each day. We all find it enjoyable to do things at our own pace. You may know older people who use their extra time gardening or going to exercise classes. Others decide to study.

Older people enjoy having the freedom to do things they couldn't before because they were working. Many older people visit lots of new places, both near to home and far away. They take advantage of the cheap rates offered to them to travel on buses and trains. You may have noticed that many places such as restaurants, movie theaters and sports arenas also give reduced prices to Senior Citizens.

Many people welcome the chance to talk about old times with friends and acquaintances or with their families.

Having retired from work, older people no longer receive a regular wage from an employer. But they do receive money back from the government. This is "Social Security." People who have planned for their retirement may also have an individual retirement fund or pension. This is to make sure they have enough money to pay their living expenses and maybe do the things they want to do. At its best, old age means that people can do things because they like to and not because they have to.

Many older people enjoy being around younger people. They like sharing their skills with them and finding out about what young people have been doing. You may love being with your grandparents, and have many good memories of days that you have spent with them. Older people who have grown-up children with families of their own often feel very proud of their grandchildren. Many grandparents become involved with taking care of the younger members of their families.

Grandparents from all over the world enjoy being with younger members of their families. Some parents tend to worry that grandparents spoil their grandchildren.

23

"What stops people from enjoying their old age?"

Old age is as much a challenge as every other part of our lives. Sometimes this challenge becomes more difficult. This may be because of the way our bodies change as we grow older. Elderly people who can no longer see well feel less confident when they are walking. Sometimes they stop trying to do things because their bodies don't work as well.

Illness can also prevent some elderly people from doing as much as they want to. When we are young, our bodies react quickly to fight illnesses. In some older people, this reaction is much slower, and the body does not repair itself as easily as it once did. In some cases, older people are forced to rely on others to help them. This can make them depressed or irritable. Some may feel they are losing their dignity or their independence. Others may not feel confident enough to ask for help. You may know an elderly person who says that he or she doesn't want to be a nuisance.

The government sets money aside for older people who have retired from work. Claiming the money involves filling out forms. Sometimes older people are confused by forms. This means that they can miss out on their rights.

If people are less able to do things than they were, time may seem to pass slowly. Some older people may be living on their own. They may find this difficult if they are used to having others around. Some are very aware that they have almost reached the end of their lives. Others are no longer able to live alone. They may move into a nursing home or into an adult residence, so that they can be better cared for.

Some older people only have enough money to get by. They cannot afford many luxuries. Some are even afraid to turn on the heating because of the money it costs, and this can be dangerous, particularly in winter. Older people aren't always aware of the money that the government sets aside for them. Advice centers can help them claim what they are due.

Extra help of many kinds is available. There are services to provide hot meals if elderly people can no longer cook for themselves. There are day centers to visit. Here older people can meet and talk with others, and there are classes and activities to take part in.

Day centers and nursing homes provide all kinds of activities to help older people get the most out of life. The picture shows a dance at a center run by elderly people themselves.

"What will I be like when I am old?"

You have probably not thought very much about what you might be like when you are old. This is not surprising. It seems such a long time away. Lots of people think it is a good idea to plan for their old age. It is impossible to predict the future, but the things we do when we are young may well have an effect on us later in life. For example, young people who are starting to smoke cigarettes should think about the fact that this may affect their lungs when they are older.

Exercise will help to keep our bodies healthy, as will eating the right foods. But health is about more than having a body that works well. Keeping in touch with others and understanding our feelings are just as vital to our well-being. Thinking about our attitudes toward ourselves and others is important. Some young people say they don't want to be old. Talking to older people and trying to understand what it means to be old can make old age seem less frightening.

We can get clues about how we will look when we are older by studying the way our parents and our grandparents look today.

"What can I do?"

In the end, whether someone is nice to know has very little to
do with how old they are. You know that no two people are
alike. This is just as true for old people too. You may know
some old people who like to talk about how things were when
they were young. Others are much more involved with what
is going on now. There are times to offer help, and times
when it is not a good idea unless you check carefully first,
particularly with strangers.

It helps to see old age as an adventure. Old people have
lived through many changes. You may not always agree with
the things they say. But by understanding and respecting
their feelings, you can help to break down the barriers put up
by ageism. You might also learn a lot!

Addresses for further information

Department of Health
and Human Services
Administration on Aging
200 Independence Avenue S.W.
Washington, DC 20201

Contact local senior citizens
centers and your city, town, or
state Department for the Aging.

30

What the words mean

adult residence is housing for older people, where a caretaker checks daily to see that all is well.

ageism is seeing elderly people as a group rather than as individuals, and expecting them to behave in a particular way.

arthritis is a disease that affects joints, making them stiff and painful.

nursing home is where older people who can no longer take care of themselves are cared for by paid workers and voluntary helpers.

pension is the money people receive once they have given up work. It may be paid by the government (Social Security), by an employer, or it may have been saved as a retirement account by people themselves during their working life.

retirement is the time when older people give up work. In this country the retirement age is 60 for women and 65 for men.

senior citizen is a person past retirement age. A senior citizen is also sometimes called a **pensioner**.

Index

Photographic Credits:

Cover and pages 6-7, 8-9, 11 bottom right, 15, 25 and 29: Marie-Helene Bradley; page 5: Paul Nightingale; page 11 top right and left and bottom left: generously donated by Olive Martin; pages 12-13 and 22: The Hutchison Library; page 16: generously donated by Mr. and Mrs. B. Krikler; page 16-17: the Robert Harding Picture Library; page 18-19: Eye Ubiquitous; pages 20-21 and 26-27: Mike Abrahams/Network Photographers.

PRINTED IN BELGIUM BY
proost
INTERNATIONAL BOOK PRODUCTION